WHEN GOD INTERVENES

by

Jean John

authorHOUSE®

AuthorHouse™ UK Ltd.
500 Avebury Boulevard
Central Milton Keynes, MK9 2BE
www.authorhouse.co.uk
Phone: 08001974150

First published by AuthorHouse 12/28/2009

ISBN: 978-1-4490-3859-5 (sc)

This book is printed on acid-free paper.

ABOUT THE BOOK

When God Intervenes is an inspiring story about a shy insecure woman who was empowered by God to carry out a big mission far beyond her own level of expectation in a needy community where people dared her to perform the task. Faced with the daunting possibility of achieving the goal, her passion and concern for people suffering the effects of mental illness drove her to pursue that mission regardless of the obstacles faced. This book is funny, honest, touching, and shows that God can hide his face for several seasons at times. Nevertheless He can be trusted in the deepest of valleys to show up and work alongside an individual that is willing to trust Him and go the distance.In doing this she also successfully managed what has now grown to become a well established and sought after organisation.

Trust in the Lord with all thine heart; and lean not unto thine own understanding. In all thy ways acknowledge him, and he shall direct thy paths.

(PROVERBS 3: 5-6)

DEDICATION

This book is dedicated to Lareisse whose kind words and actions brought renewed hope for better days to come and Vera who encouraged me throughout this mission and to the numerous volunteers, supporters and colleagues for their support.

CONTENTS

THE BEGINNING OF A JOURNEY   1

HOUSE PRAYER MEETINGS   13

PERSECUTION   21

THE BIRTH OF AN ORGANISATION   27

WAYSIDE   33

     AWAY DAYS   36

THE RESTRUCTURING OF THE PROJECT   39

     HEALTH PROJECT   40

THE DECLINE   43

CHATSWORTH ROAD   49

     GOD'S PROVIDENCE   53

NEW DEVELOPMENTS   59

     CHARITY SHOP   59

     OLD PEOPLES HOME OUTREACH   60

     THE SUNSHINE PROJECT   61

     OVERSEAS OUTREACH PROJECT   62

     INSHAPE PARTNERSHIP   64

THE SUSTAINING POWER OF GOD   67

The Beginning of a Journey

On spring bank holiday, May 1987, as I left home to walk the short distance to catch the coach to Derbyshire: the day seemed like any other day of the year. The neighbourhood was quiet and calm as people were still asleep. On this particular day I was among several members of our church party who were attending the final celebration weekend convention held yearly at Cliff College.

Cliff College was established in 1883 and provides theological and practical training in Christian evangelism, service and ministry for Methodism and the wider Church to students of all denominations and many countries. The College is situated in Hope Valley in Derbyshire, in the beautiful Peak District National Park

My only knowledge of the place was that one of my church sister's, Carole, had studied there for a year and had invited others from our church to attend the various yearly conventions. This particular day trip was organised by one of our Local preachers, Mathilda Biam-Small, who for several years had frequented the celebrations and had often taken groups of young people there. So here I was on my way expecting nothing special just happy to be going outside London; but this journey would prove to be the beginning of a new chapter in my life.

Our journey started at 7.00am, and was estimated to take three hours but took several hours due to the heavy traffic. We had hoped to arrive in time to attend the first of the seminars held outside on the Terrace, but by the time we arrived this activity was already in progress. As soon as we arrived we were confronted with the view of hundreds of cars, caravans, tents, and numerous coaches. There were those on foot walking from both direction and people seemed to be coming from everywhere.

We were so taken up by the crowds that no one noticed that Mathilda had mysteriously vanished. We were strangers to the area, so it was with some trepidation that we ventured out of the coach to go in search for Mathilda. Some went to the nearest tent, whilst others including myself found the Terrace.

The Terrace was an area located between two main buildings of the College, which evolved from an 18th century Manor House. Here, the service was conducted in the open air with a make shift rostrum. Situated on the hill above, and overlooking the Terrace was the most beautiful arranged flower gardens I've seen. A wall separated the Terrace from the garden, which was accessible by several rows of steps. As we entered we could see that the area was already packed to capacity. People were sitting in every available space possible - the garden walls, and even on the ground among the flowerbeds.

A group of singers led the worship, which was very vibrant. From the expression on the people's faces you could see they were happy to be there. They were smiling; more over they were very welcoming and made every effort to make space for us to find a spot. Their singing was joyful and boisterous; their entire bodies were caught up in the act of worship. Some raised their hands in adoration, whilst others clasped their hands as if in prayer and occasionally people yelled Hallelujah, Amen, thank you Jesus. This was unusual to me, however I settled down unstirred by the emotions of the people around me and waited for the preacher to be announced.

Soon after the preacher began to speak it was as if he had mysteriously picked me out from among the crowd of people. His message seemed to address me and every word spoken made a demand of me. His voice penetrated into my entire being, which made me feel conscious that the congregation too was aware that his message was directed to me. This preacher was making a demand on my life telling me I had certain duties to perform in the church, and I certainly was not prepared to get involved there. By now I was beginning to feel very angry and had a great urge to escape. I simply switched off and went to a pity party with myself thinking of my own sad state of affair of the heart, the breakdown of my marriage, which was very painful. How was I going to cope? What would become of me? These were a few of my questions. I was not particularly good company and was getting rather critical of this group of people who seemed so full of themselves. Clapping, smiling even looking happy in Church: whatever next? I thought.

The church where I worshiped was quiet in contrast to Cliff College. In fact, all four churches in the circuit were quiet and reserved. Our church in particular could be full on Sundays and yet you'll be forgiven if you were passing in the street for believing that only a few people worshipped there. The church was made up of mainly older people, although young families worshipped there; also, the structure of the services were more likely to attract the older generation. The singing was soft and it was one of those places where no matter how hard you listen you could not distinguish the voice of the other person standing next to you. Peradventure someone came to church whose voice could be heard above the pitch of the others everyone turned to see who had violated the sacredness of the atmosphere.

This place was certainly different and instead of welcoming that form of worship I rejected it because of its energy.

At the end of the meeting we made our way in search of somewhere to sit and eat. Once outside I was made even more aware of the vast numbers of people who had come to the convention.

The multitude of worshippers filled the park as far as the eye could see. They were coming from the upper tent, the Terrace, the children's meeting, the big tent, and the lower tent. People were ascending and descending the hill, some were sitting in groups on the grass at the top of the hill others were sitting around their caravans. The beauty of the colours of their attire amid the green grass and the surrounding hills was magnificent to behold. The sound of music mingled with the voices of children at play filled the air, and I could picture a biblical scene with Jesus on the hillside of Galilee and a multitude of people coming there to hear him speak. I had never been in a place as this before. The scene was mesmerising, as I stood and gazed at the beautiful Derbyshire hills I said truly: *"God is in this place"*.

As we sat down for lunch the feeling of unease came again. There is definitely something spooky about this place I thought. The message about getting involved in the mission of the church was being transmitted in my brain and I was hearing it loud and clear so much so that I felt the urge to escape once more.

On our arrival we had seen several adverts to a carnival in Chesterfield, so I thought I'd go there and get back in time for the coach back to London. After getting several others interested we went to make enquiries on how to get to Chesterfield, to our disappointment we found that the buses came every hour and that we wouldn't have enough time to get there and back for our homeward journey. Frustrated, I decided to spend the rest of the evening sitting on the coach. As I pondered over the situation my thoughts went on the bookshop up the hill. I loved reading and thought it would be good to browse around in the shop and see if anything on display caught my fancy. Perhaps I'd find a good book to read whilst I waited for the others to return for the journey home. Feeling more relaxed I began the short walk in search of the shop. On the way to the Terrace I remembered passing a sign that showed the position of the shop, so I went directly there. I was only there a few minutes when I was approached by Vera, a friend who had arrived to the weekend celebrations ahead of us. She was quite happy to meet up with me, but somehow she seemed to be in a hurry and quickly pointed out two books she thought I should read. Together we went to the checkout and paid for the books, the *Holy Spirit and you* and *Nine 0 clock in the Morning*.

Taking me by the hand she said we must hurry or we won't get a seat. We went to the lower tent to hear Rev Colin

Urquhart. Vera had heard him speak a few times before as he was one of the main speakers for the weekend event. In her excitement she told me all she knew about him. He was an Anglican Priest previously, but he was now an Evangelist and: *"You've got to hear him"* she insisted. I had nothing against this man of God, but I was not particularly interested to sit amongst those who instead of sitting quietly and listen to the preacher respond with hallelujah and amen and this Jesus thing. *"Why were they saying his name so often?"* I came to the conclusion that they were new to church and thought they had to say his name. In my heart I was protesting: *"No I'm sorry, but I'm not going."* but I did not want to let her down.

All my life I've tried to please others; never wanting people to think badly of me, after all Vera was enjoying the conference. She happily told me what I had missed over the past few days. The bible study, morning prayer meetings, speakers, walking along the prayer paths, the new friends made etc. I could not tell her how uncomfortable I felt being there so I went along quite unwillingly to the lower tent. I did not know at that time that my life would never be the same.

Up to that period of time my life was a boring one. I was a very sensitive person, who took offence for the simplest of things said about me, kept very much to myself and I did not make good company. This meant I had no friends and was the worst off for being lonely and isolated.

I was brought up in a small country village in the Caribbean in a family that kept very much to themselves, which meant I had a very reserved upbringing. We lived across the road from the Methodist church that my family attended religiously every Sunday. The little chapel was used for Christian worship and sufficed as a school that provided education to children from the age of five to 16. My village and those from other areas also used this chapel/school.

The chapel was a hive of community events, as it provided various social activities organised by missionaries who taught several Irish and English folk songs.

I was a weak child and suffered from some common ailment or other including asthma that plagued me regularly especially in the rainy season. This condition kept me from participating in most of these activities and attending school regularly; and I was absent for several months of the year. However, by living nearby I was able to work from home so in spite of the setbacks I was bright and succeeded in each stage of the school exams.

I was very shy and particularly choosy in my dress sense. Unlike other girls of my age who wore ordinary below the knee dresses I liked mine ankle length. I also felt unable to have my arm, chest and back exposed and people referred to me among other things as being old fashioned, stupid, and why can't you be as everyone else? I was constantly being criticised and felt very unloved, rejected, and condemned just for being me.

As I grew up these feelings continued and I felt that I would never succeed in life, as I had never been given any encouragement. However, deep down I longed to be some body. After leaving school I was sent to study pitman typing and book keeping. On Arriving Here, in England at the age of 20, I continued my studies in typing and office practice, including several life courses but this fear of rejection continued with me throughout and even though I had acquired several certificates of distinctions I was unable to make a career in any of them through fear of not being good enough.

As a young girl I dreamt of marrying a gentle, loving and kind man but alas this was just a folly of a simple-minded girl who had no exposure to the world at large. People like me from a small village in a small island have no knowledge of places outside the vicinity where she lives, has no real life experiences and could only make believe. So my dreams were unrealistic, and after trying to hold on for the sake of the children the marriage ended after 20 years. So here I was at Cliff College with various emotional feelings. I felt alone, abandoned, rejected and thought that there was definitely no hope for me finding my dreams come true.

Now I was hearing testimonies of people who had similar life experiences. In communicating their life story they told of a loving father who came to their rescue when they called, they spoke of heartaches, pain, rejection, abuse suffered in silence and the bitterness they harboured in their hearts and of the release and freedom found as they invited Jesus into their lives.

I had never been at a place where I've heard of wonderful things like these. I felt myself wanting to be free from my pain, and gradually I was opening up but remained sceptical.

These were young people: I was now 43 years old and I still felt rejected, unloved, humiliated, scorned etc. *"God, I will like to have a testimony, but why are they talking about Jesus so much."* I thought. Up till then I very rarely heard people calling on the name of Jesus or even asserting that he did something for them. Were these people real? Again, I felt uneasy and wanted to make my exit, as I was about to do so a young man sitting somewhere along the pew decided to get up and beckoned me to his seat. We exchanged places just at the point of introducing the speaker the Rev. Colin Urquhart. Perhaps I'll stay and listen to him after all. He came from the Church of England they won't dare express themselves whilst he's speaking.

He invited people to give their lives to Christ. Even though I was brought up in the church, had attended Sunday school regularly, at the age of 12 attended reception classes, learnt my catechism and made a commitment to follow Christ and was finally received as a member of the Methodist Church this didn't feel right for me. As I reflected on these things I became aware of a headache that I had all day. I was beginning to feel miserable again, I thought about the difficulties of my life and of my longing to find peace, and happiness. As far as I knew peace could only be acquired in death, right now my life seemed to be of no real value what so ever. In fact, I was fed up of life.

As the minister prayed for people to accept Jesus as Lord of their lives I finally thought I might as well give him my life. I needed his intervention and without any more resistance I closed my eyes and said: *"Jesus you can have my life. I don't want it anymore. Have it. Here, catch."* I threw myself in the hand of Jesus and as he caught hold of me immediately I felt as though a large burden had fallen off my shoulders and I was filled with the most wonderful sense of peace imaginable. From that moment I had no recollection of the people standing there in the tent with me.

The Marquee that contained hundreds of people suddenly seemed to be empty except for the Spirit of God at my side and me. Suddenly I could hear the preacher speaking in tongues, but in English I heard a voice calling me by name (Jean), and telling me what he wanted me to do. I wondered how he knew my name and how did he find me among such a crowd. When at last I was able to open my eyes I found that the people were all there and I knew beyond a shadow of a doubt that something miraculous had taken place. Even the atmosphere seemed changed; inside me was a hushed silence. My very soul was at peace and from that moment I had no recollection of the rest of the service. I was simply lost in wonder pondering over the mysteries of God.

I've heard the phrase born again but I had no idea how this came about now I had experienced a change and I suddenly knew. The person who stood there in the spot where I stood was not the same creature now. A transaction had taken place and I knew I was born again. *"Why didn't I learn about this mystery before? Did every one in the tent have the same experience?"* I was deep in thought and was not aware of the time until a tap on the shoulder by one of my colleagues made me realise it was time to leave the meeting for the three hour journey home.

On the way people were engaging in conversation on the coach talking about their day. I, however, remained silent still lost in wonder, love and praise. On arriving home that evening I was met by an acquaintance that commented on the glow upon my countenance. *"What happen to you she asked? There is a glow on your face."* I found it hard to explain what had happened, but in my own way I said there is something strange about the place (I now know that the something strange was the presence of Jesus) it reminded me of biblical times when Jesus went up on a hill to preach and the vast multitude of people that went from everywhere to hear him and you could see yourself as one of the crowd.

I went in my room and fell on my knees and prayed. I opened up my bible my fingers fell on John chapter one I began to read:

In the beginning was the word and the word was with God and the word was God.

I was led to verse 14

and the word was made flesh

at that point the words on the page seem to come alive they were lifting off the page and moving about as if in a dance. I opened up my eyes wide in wonder—*"What on earth is happening to me?"* I asked. Then I heard myself saying loudly: *"My God Jesus is the living word made flesh."* Until that moment I did not know this fact, even though I attended church regularly. As I ponder upon the event of the day the words of two hymns came to me, one was by John Newton:

*Amazing grace how sweet the sound that save a
wretch like me
I once was lost but now I'm found was blind but
now I see.*

*Through many dangers toils and snares I have
already come
God's grace has brought me safe thus far
And he will lead me home*

(John Newton)

The other hymn was by Charles Wesley:

*And can it be that I should gain
An interest in the Saviour's blood?
Died he for me, who caused his pain
For me, who him to death pursued
Amazing love how can it be
That thou, my God, shouldst die for me?*

*Long my imprisoned spirit lay
Fast bound in sin and nature's night
Thine eye diffused a quickening ray
I woke, the dungeon flamed with light*

My chains fell off, my heart was free
I rose, went forth, and followed thee

No condemnation now I dread
Jesus and all in him is mine
Alive in him, my living head
And clothed in righteousness divine
Bold I approach the eternal throne
And claim the crown through Christ,
my own.

(CHARLES WESLEY)

I've sung those hymns in church since childhood without understanding their true meaning. Now for the first time I understood the hearts of the men who penned those hymns. They too had met with the risen Christ and had left something powerful behind for other people to reflect on the grace of God. I felt free, and was later to comment that before I went to Cliff College I was a sluggish caterpillar with a diet of cabbage leaves, but by the time I left I'd become a butterfly with a totally new diet prepared for me.

The next morning as I set out for work the world seemed to be a different place. Instead of hearing the noisy traffic on the street I was aware of the singing of birds in the trees. I took notice of the flowers in the garden, which seemed to portray the beauty of God in a way that I'd not seen before. In fact the journey that I took to work each day had never seemed as beautiful as it was that morning. I was bubbling up with joy. I called out good morning to every one I met and said have a good day.

I was so happy I began to sing and I found myself saying praise God, Hallelujah, amen, thank you Jesus. I was behaving just like the people at Cliff. I was definitely going to be good company from now on.

That night I got out my typewriter and began to write to Ken, my Superintend minister, asking why we don't rejoice in church. I told him of my experience of worship at Cliff

College. The following Sunday he came up to me and asked if he could come to my house to discuss the letter. On arrival he asked what inspired me to write to him, and I gave him my testimony. Ken was wonderful and explained the disappearing and reappearing congregation in the meeting to me.

He said: "You had a most wonderful conversion experience and it is usually difficult for the person themselves to communicate meetings with God. You were at one with God that's why you felt alone in the marquee; you were standing in the very presence of God. What are you going to do now? How about preaching?"

"I don't know the bible" I replied.

"He will teach you. Just pray about it."

A few days after that prayer I was woken up with a voice saying: Read Mark 16:15. Turning to my bible I read:

And he said unto them Go ye into all the world and preach the gospel to every creature.

This confirmed what Ken suggested and led to my being trained and commissioned as a Methodist Local Preacher in 1989, but things would not go smoothly and I would leave the fellowship of this church for a number of years to come.

HOUSE PRAYER MEETINGS

My life was never going to be the same after my experience at Cliff. Gone was the fickle-minded individual that lived to earn the approval of those who were most unpleasant to me. No more was I going to be afraid of the world and its inhabitants, nor the fears that paralysed and condemned me over the years. I felt free at last to look people in the eye and express myself in a clear and positive manner. God had truly transformed my life and personality giving me a new approach to life. I was enjoying this newfound freedom.

Over the years when grey shadows blurred my sight I had a subtle dislike of myself as I had taken on the caricature of the person others had pertained me to be. And I abhor this image, deep down in my inner self I felt as though the real me was in hibernation. Here I was at the age of 43 meeting up with myself for the first time, liking what I saw and being introduced to the real me.

Finding whom I was revealed hidden skills and unused abilities buried in ashes unrecognised over the years. A new vitality emerged enabling me to perform duties, which previously was too strenuous for my frail body to handle and opened up a brand new world for me. I also found my voice, what a joy this was to speak without fear of being ridiculed just for being me. I was free to express my opinions even if they were different from other people's point of view. At least I was now strong enough to be heard and God would use my life to have a great impact on the lives of countless individuals.

This newfound way of life however had its disadvantages; some people seeing the dynamic change likened it to insanity and described me as: 'gone mad'. Some certified this as fact because not only was I seen in the company of the mentally ill and other people seen as outcasts I also welcomed them in my home.

Before my conversion as many women of my age I was very house-proud always cleaning, polishing, dusting etc. I made sure nothing was out of place. The front room was the place for guests and the doors were kept shut. I would sit there on occasions and admire my home feeling proud. No way would I have invited any and every body into my home. Imagine my horror when God spoke one day and said start a prayer meeting: *"Where? I haven't got a spare room, so where could I hold these meetings? Here in this room, surely not in my front room I protested - yes in this room"*. After much deliberations, however, I gave up my precious room never to have it as my pride and joy again soon I would write my name in the dust on the furniture as the welfare of needy people became more important to me than material things.

The first thing I did was to inform Ken my minister about my intention to start a prayer meeting at home. He encouraged me and said he would give his support if needed. He took great interest in what was going on spiritually in my life and asked that I keep him informed of all that God was doing among us. The first prayer meeting began on Thursday 5th November 1987, six months after my conversion. There were two people beside myself, Mathilda who had become my mentor, and one other person. Mathilda presided over the first few meetings allowing me time to gain confidence. Soon I was able to take over and by the third month 38 people was in attendance.

The vision God gave was that of people coming from all traditions of the Christian faith. Some with positions within their churches others to develop themselves for leadership. And so they came, the Methodists, Baptists, Church of England, Pentecostals, Catholics, Adventists Independent etc. We met each week for fellowship and prayer and left behind our various traditions and contradictions and focused on Christ our saviour.

These meetings were different from the traditional church prayer meetings.They were to be a means of helping people know the love of Christ Jesus and enable them to build confidence enough to share their opinions in open discussions. God wanted me to demonstrate to them that they were special, appreciated, and loved. When we met I took particular interest in each person by greeting them affectionately and encouraged them to talk about their week. I showed people that God was very much interested in their social life as well as their spiritual life and that it was okay to talk about our fears, doubts, disappointments etc. In the early meetings many people were unaccustomed to such gatherings and found it difficult to express their true feelings. However, within a few weeks people began to lose their inhibitations and open up.

This sharing of our lives gave people a new freedom to carry every thing to God and many conservative people were openly expressing their faith in a positive manner for the first time in their lives.

Friendships developed through the time of openly sharing our lives in fellowship. People found new hope and meaning to their lives and found it easier to cope with their situations. God had created an environment where people felt loved and cared for. There was a sense of joy among us. God worked miraculously in the meetings; people were getting healed from various illnesses, as the prayers were very effectual. People were also witnesses to changes occurring day by day in the lives of individuals. Those who couldn't pray before were now able to do so whilst others found new relationships with the Lord.

One evening the meeting was going on as usual. I was reading a Psalm when suddenly I became aware of someone breathing air in me. I continued to read the psalm from the beginning again this time I found myself reading in the first person. Whilst I read the breath continued to pour in me and I was being inflated like a balloon. As I filled up, my fingers and toes felt like they were expanding and waves of power were coming out of them. My whole body felt like a circuit sending out electricity. I was becoming more and more inflated and could not feel the floor I was standing on and I felt lifted above the ground. The Spirit of God was breathing air in me. I was petrified by now, as it seemed certain that I would go pop at any moment. I said: *"Stop! Stop! I have enough"*. When this activity ceased I was instructed to lay a hand on the people. As I did so, I could not feel the area where my hand was placed. It was as though God was just using my hand to touch them himself. I began to walk across the floor, and once again I could not feel the ground that I was walking on instead I felt as though I was walking on air. That night God had placed upon me a powerful anointing to minister to the multitude of broken people that he would send for healing and deliverance in his name.

After the event of that night the word spread even further and people now began to turn up during the day and a new project was in the making before I knew it my home had become an open door to the community. I packed in my job as a care Assistant and made myself available to those who came.

A new group of people began to turn up at my door now. They were referred by relatives who thought that prayer would help their conditions. They were suffering from alcohol addiction, and mental illness. Those with mental distress were diagnosed with manic depression, schizophrenia, mild depression and so on. Some had poor social skills, others irritating mannerisms. At that time many incidences of violent attack on members of the community was attributed to people suffering mental disorders and relatives and acquaintances were concerned for my safety in associating myself with these people termed 'dangerous'. I, on the other hand, had no such reservations for myself instead I wanted to help them overcome the power of the illness that had dominated their lives, which left them being looked upon as inferior in society. A society that was bent on isolating them even further.

God had created them in his image and likeness, but the environment, circumstances and the wider society was instrumental in bringing about this situation they found themselves in. I found that the way we behave to others could have a lasting effect on their mental wellbeing. We as human beings have no regard for one another. We pronounce what ever words come into our minds without thinking of the hurt and pain the effect could have. We fail to realise that when we speak harsh words in anger to our brothers and sisters we are actually sending out missles to wound the target. After the cruel words had taken effect on a person, society then disowns the victims.

I had no special qualifications to give expert support to these inidividuals, except that I had gained a City and Guild certificate in Community Studies. This two-year full-time study of life from birth to retirement had given me some insight into the various conditions that presented themselves in these individuals. This enabled me to use those acquired skills to give good counsel with relation to the importance of taking medication, getting them to talk about their feelings (talk therapy) and involving them in group work, so as to help them to become motivated.

Society was scared of these people, but I saw something much deeper than fear. I saw human beings under oppression and desperately needing the love, care and understanding of the church. These were timid and frightened individuals whose lives were deteriorating rapidly and who had no means of helping themselves.

Welcoming these broken people into the fellowship was in itself the best remedy for them. God had given me a remedy of love, compassion and affection to embrace the broken hearted, and this was sufficient to meet what ever needs they had.

I approached them with the strongest weapon known to man, the power of love. Love has a tendency to improve the lives of every man by penetrating even the hardest and coldest of hearts, and show them a better way. I entered into their suffering and empathised with them.

I knew what it was like to feel lost, helpless and without hope. I too had gone through years of suffering from depression. I was too scared to let anyone know the torment of my mind, and frightened to speak of the dark night of the soul when suicidal thoughts filled the very core of my being. In those days/nights of deep despair I often cried out in the dark in silence and many days I would feel the tears falling inward, as rain drops upon my heart so much so that at times I feared my heart would drown in a sea of tears.

Listening to these people, I seemed to get a glimpse into their situations. Many times all I'd do is give them a hug and a kind word and the tears would fall from their eyes, as they open up and find release. The cure for broken and hurt people is a remedy that has to be administered by another human being. This remedy is not something that could be manufactured in a laboratory, bought from a chemist shop and taken three times a day. Love should be given freely and administered in the form of kind words, and deeds. The power of love and prayer broke down many barriers, as I gave them the assurance that God was bigger than their biggest need, and that his love for them was everlasting. Having welcomed them as individuals needing mercy and compassion they were shown courtesy and treated with respect. God quietly did the rest. He restored their lives helping them to regain confidence and self esteem, so much so that they would offer mutual support to others later.

Rapid changes was witnessed in the lives of these particular individuals. The miraculous transformation was so powerful that it became a living testimony to those who knew them previously. Around this time enquiries were made to get the house bound included for ministry and within six months from the start of the first prayer meeting the telephone became a vital link to connect this group of people to receive prayer.

People called in expressing their loneliness and isolation from the outside world. Many were church members prior to their illnesses, and missed having fellowship with others. Vera and I made arangements to visit these people in their homes in an effort to bring the gospel and thus offer renewed hope and reassurance of the love of Christ Jesus.

We did our outreach on Fridays usually starting in Hackney then travelled out in the evening to conduct prayers with families. Sometimes up to 20 people were present, as neighbours were invited to join the family. There was a hunger in people's lives and they responded to the gospel message. As their situations changed they gave our telephone number to other family members in the country. People now began to call for prayer from Birmingham, Wolverhampton, and Reading. They also called from oversees from America, Canada, Jamaica, and Grenada. Healing and deliverances were taking place on the telephone. Testimonies came from everywhere.

Bible Study

I was trained to be a counsellor in the Billy Graham mission in 1989. Through that mission we started what was called prayer triplet. This involved three people meeting regularly to pray for unsaved friends/family/acquaintances within a short time other people came along and eventually it grew to 24 people. This was later turned into a bible study group. One young woman started attending and she brought along several others, many of whom had walked away from their churches through criticism by elders/members. We showed them love and accepted them as individuals. They found space to ask questions, and soon they were expressing their love for the Lord and progressed in the faith. Finding their faith again they returned to their fellowships and some even entered bible college to study for the ministry. Today several young people who attended are in prominent ministries of their own.

PERSECUTION

Serving God can be dangerous even in this society. People are being persecuted simply for laying down their lives for the gospel. At the age of 14 I had accepted Jesus as my Lord and Saviour, but through the lack of teachings was unable to grow spiritually. For years, I felt my life was'nt what it should be, and that there was something more to being a christian than just going to church on Sundays. Now that I found new meaning to my life and had given up everything to care for those who were less fortunate in society, it was as though I had changed my religion. I had found a new and vibrant way of expressing my faith in Jesus Christ and this had caused a great offence, as I began to encounter persecution as I've never experienced before.

Jesus said,"Think not that I am come to send peace on earth. I came not to send peace, but a sword. For I am come to set a man at variance against his father, and the daughter against her mother, and the daughter-in-law against her mother-in-law.

And a man's foes shall be they of his own household".

(MATT 10:34-36)

21

Jesus did not come to bring the kind of peace that will smooth out differences and instil harmony instead conflicts and disagreements will come between those who choose to follow Christ and those who don't.

Before surrendering my life to Christ no one had ever referred to me as being evil. Instead, people spoke well of me. Now that I had been sanctified in Christ I was accused of being evil, worthless, insane, and even being a devil worshipper.

People looked upon the work I was called to as being of no particular value and began to ignore me. Close acquaintances began to avoid me also, strong family ties were broken, whilst others even refused to hear my testimony saying I was mad.

Rumour after rumour spread about me; even throughout the church. This was a time of great confusion for me. I found it hard to understand how the very people whom I've shared worship with could turn against me for doing the will of God.

Surrendering my life to Christ made me see that society wants nothing to do with those who consciously make a decision to follow Christ. I was made to feel like I'd committed an unpardonable sin against them for seeking God in a deeper way. Wasn't this what the church was all about? A great sense of loss filled my very being, but it led me to turn to the only one that promised never to fail or abandon me. The one who promised to take me up though mother and father forsake me. Throughout this period in time Vera encouraged me throughout the ordeal and it seemed as though she was the only person who believed in the work being done. Looking back I would say those were the times when God seemed closer to me as I kept my faith in God through constant prayer and bible study and was able to come through positively. I had made a conscious decision to follow Christ and come what may I was determined to go on.

My two eldest boys however lost their jobs as a direct result of the upheaval in the family, and this was a very difficult time for us in terms of finances. Because I had given up my job freely I had no income and apart from the mortgage, which was taken care of by my estranged husband, I had no income to live, and received no assistance from social services.

One day the dreaded letters came to remind me that the amenities hadn't been paid and that they would be cut off on a certain date. I cried out to the Lord: *"Where do you expect me to find the finances to pay these bills. After all it was you who asked me to pack up my job. What am I to do?"* I had said what was on my heart, but I never expected a reply. I was definitely mistaken to think that way. I heard:

"Jean Who do you think I am?

"I stammered I-I-I don't know."

"How do you see me?"

The question demanded an answer and I really did not have any. However, I said:

"A man."

"What Kind of man?"

This was certainly becoming too much for me as I was quivering inside. Quick as a flash I thought Jesus was a tall man, so I said:

"A tall man."

After this reply I was to be taken into a place of awe and great wonder that would change my whole narrow outlook of God as the Creator, sustainer and preserver of my life. God would instil in me a tremendous ability to put faith into action that would baffle the wise.

Fancy calling God a man, he certainly did not expect anything else from one such as I who knew very little about him. I often wonder if Church ministers knew that the vast majority of people in their congregations have very limited knowledge/understanding of God even though they attend church regularly. Most people do not read the bible, most churches do not encourage people to join bible study groups and without these relevant and important activities how are they to have knowledge of God? This was very real in my situation and I could not explain whom God is. However, in his mercy and grace he will become my teacher and reveal to me things beyond my natural understanding.

This dialogue between God and me continued and it was his turn to speak. His response to him being a tall man was:

"And my spirit moved upon the face of the waters".

I had read Genesis 1 many times at Sunday school and as an adult but it said nothing in particular to me. This time, however, I immediately became aware of an enormous 'being' spreading out throughout the universe. This being was so vast that he filled my home with his presence and I could think of no words to describe the vastness. The very partitions of my home seemed to disappear, as the walls could not contain him. King Solomon said:

"The house which I build is great for great is our God above all gods. But who is able to build him an house, seeing the heaven and heaven of heavens cannot contain him"?

(2 CHRON 2:5-6)

Sitting in my chair it felt as though I was standing, but that I had shrunk to nothingness in the presence of this all mighty being (God). I felt like a speck of dust upon the ground. I was petrified and cried out in my soul Woe is me for I am undone. I thought if my children came into the house they will not be able to see me and walk on me, as I would be invisible to them and that will be the end of me.

When the vision was over I scampered up to my room to look in the mirror to see whether I was all there, as I still had a sense of being consumed but there I was in my natural stature. I sat down upon the bed and pondered upon the almighty God and said.

"Thine O, Lord, is the greatness, and the power, and the glory, and the victory, and the majesty

for all that is in the heaven and in the earth is thine, thine is the kingdom, 0 Lord, and thou art exalted as head above all"

(1 CHRON 29;11)

I had limited God according to my limited understanding and he had opened up the eye of my understanding and had shown me there are no limitations with him. He'd shown me that he cannot be located at any one place, but that he is available at all times and in all places at the same time.

As a child I could not understand how God could be everywhere. I believed that there were times when he was busy at another place and could not see me. I remember saying to my great Aunt: *"I could hide in a cupboard and he would not see me."* Unlike me the Psalmist knew differently when he wrote:

Whither shall I go from thy spirit? Or whither shall I flee from thy presence? If I ascend up into heaven, thou art there if I make my bed in hell, behold, thou art there. If I take the wings of the morning, and dwell in the uttermost parts of the sea even there shall thy hand lead me and thy right hand shall hold me

(PSALM 139: 7-10)

God had demonstrated his power and might and I would spend the rest of my life to operate through faith in this knowledge of the Sovereign God.

After this encounter I saw God in a new light. I saw him as my all in all. As provider he made ways for me to pay the bills and I had never gone without a meal. That Christmas we went carolling with other church folks at the local hospital. I caught sight of myself in a floor length mirror and saw that my coat looked shabby, as it had done its time. I had no means of buying one and didn't think much about it. Christmas came and on Boxing Day I was presented with a large packet, on opening it I found I had been given a beautiful coat; that same

25

day, I was presented with another large packet yes another coat. God had provided two coats; one for church and one for every day wear. I had not even asked God to provide for this need but he acted on my behalf, which reminded me that Jesus said:

> *"Therefore I say unto you take no thought for your life, what ye shall eat, or what ye shall drink; nor yet for your body, what ye shall put on, is not the life more than meat, and the body than raiment?"*
>
> (Matt 6:25)

True to God's word every need was taken care of in the most remarkable way. Every problem was sorted he even restored the broken relationships, years later my accusers were to personally congratulate me on the impact the organisation made to the community work. This proves that God can be trusted to act on our behalf.

4

THE BIRTH OF AN ORGANISATION

Spiritual needs were gradually being met within my home through Christian fellowship, culturally sensitive advice, prayer, and bible study but much more needed to be done.

Social exclusion, injustice and inequality were widely experienced. Serious poverty was prevalent, whole families were unemployed, others lived in bad housing conditions, suffered from stress, and remained lonely and isolated in their homes. These people felt trapped in a recurring cycle of stress/depression and hopelessness. Those situations also contributed greatly to the deterioration of mental ill health experienced by many members of the community.

Apart from the outreach work Vera gave a few hours after bible study before going to work in the local hospital where she worked as a nurse, but much more help was needed.

We decided to call a meeting to find out what the people wanted. They voiced their concern about the impact the economic decline was having on the lives of local people. The situation cried out for a community centre that would take persons physical, social, and spiritual needs into consideration and provide care for the whole person.

It was at this point that the seriousness of the situation was fully realized and we set about seeking ways for further development. God directed us to fundraise through jumble sales and Gospel Concerts. The first of these yearly concerts was held in April 1989.

Several people were involved in organizing the concert. Apart from Vera and myself there were Carole, Mathilda, Mr Channer, and Harry who invited some young people from his church.

God orchestrated the whole event as no other could. He gave direction as to the content/direction of the event e.g.; there were scripture passages, recitations, and testimonies. There were gospel and traditional church songs being performed by choirs, duets and soloists. The event was staged by people of all ages and included various churches.

We invited people from our churches and the venue was packed. Ken, my church minister, was to comment: "Never before have I seen such unity among church People". The presence of God was awesome in that church and many people gave their lives to the Lord that evening. This activity was to continue yearly for the next 12 years. Together with conferences held they acted as means as evangelism.

After the first concert event a lady who worked with the Local Authority was referred to us. She was going through a difficult time in her life and was broken mentally, spiritually, and psychologically. Vera and I spent many hours nurturing and reassuring her of God's mercy and compassion for her life. I then began to accompany her on the long and exhausting journey to visit her mentally ill son in hospital in Broadmore. I began to understand the loneliness experienced by countless mothers sitting in the carriage of a train filled with people yet feeling all alone and isolated with no one there to offer companionship on their lonely journey. Each time I make a trip to travel as a friend/companion I knew that through that simple act of mercy God was at work bringing healing and mending broken lives. In time and with God's help she became strong and offered her expertise in the structuring of the organization.

The Organisation was called Christian Fellowship and registered as a charity in 1990.

We extended the services to include a luncheon club one day per week and operated from the Methodist Church hall where I worshipped in Chatsworth Road E5. By this time, Ken, the minister had left to work in another church and we had a new minister. Both the minister (Pat) and his wife were very supportive. Apart from attending the prayer meetings, Pat set up meetings for student doctors from St Bartholomew's hospital to visit and engage with the elderly. He also referred people to the lunch club, which meant new people were joining week after week. We had limited funds and could only manage to purchase a few pounds of poultry and vegetables, which was not enough to feed every body so we decided to have a waiting list.

One particular night we met specifically to pray for meat, as this was the most expensive item on the shopping list and I felt that God wanted us to be able to feed all who came to the lunch club. The next day the doorbell rang and one of the people standing there said that the Lord had woken her up that morning and instructed her to purchase a quantity of meat and take it to me. She asked for one of my sons to help her take them in. I found this request strange, as there were two of them already available. Imagine my surprise when all three people kept coming in with boxes upon boxes containing meat. Shocked by the sight I began to jump up and down crying and laughing all at the same time. I said: "Where am I to store these things?" Julie hung her head and looked at me with her mouth open and said: "What's the matter with you sister, why are you so amazed? You needed meat for the club didn't you?"

The consignment contained various cuts of lamb, chicken, and beef and amounted to 40 pounds in weight of each variety, plus several joints of lamb and beef and a box of chicken. My freezer was small and I didn't know how I was going to find storage. Julie and her companion suggested that I call and ask acquaintances to help with the refrigeration. They themselves took away several boxes to store for us and we were able to find people willing to help. God had showed up again in the most remarkable way. With this amount of provision we were able to accommodate and feed all who came for months upon months. Things seemed to be going smoothly. That Christmas we had 60 people in attendance at the Christmas party.

However, after our first year things began to change. The church wanted the hall for a youth club and we were told not to make ourselves too comfortable there. We had gone to the church because it was not in use. We had spent hours cleaning and making it presentable, and thought we would be there for some time but this was not to be. What were we to do?

The clientele of people we worked with was not particularly favourable in society, and there was a lot of stigma about mental illness. Apart from this we recently had a group of young adults. These young people although discharged from hospital looked really ill. At times they could be seen twitching their faces. Some would be so bad that tears came from their eyes in the process because of the bad side effects of the medication they were taking. I had great compassion for them and cared for their welfare greatly. I knew then that we had to find other means of supporting them; we just couldn't let them down. I began to attend every meeting possible to gain information of the various services in Hackney around mental health issues, to educate the community about this illness in an effort to break down the stigma around mental health issues.

We organise workshops on this topic, went on training courses and took up membership with all the various voluntary sector organisations in an effort to gain support that would better equip us to meet the needs of this client group.

In an effort to fundraise we organised jumble sales, Caribbean evenings and barbeque events. We baked cakes and sold them at Christmas bazaar and so on. Catering for community groups events, salvaged discarded items from skips, took clippings from plants and would go out in the garden in the rain to stick the cuttings in the soil so that we could get some plants to sell. We also began to raise small amounts of funds from trusts.

All this time there were those who continue to refer to me as being worthless whilst others asked if I knew what I was taking on. What about insurance, premises, renovation, staff etc., and what made me think I could carry out the task?

The comments brought back memories to a particular time of suffering in my life when someone tried to dishearten me.

At the age of 16 I started attending commercial school studying typing and book keeping not long after beginning the study I developed an ulcer on my foot and as a result was laid aside for several years unable to walk and hopped around the house.

As time progressed my friends abandoned me. I felt deserted and rejected, and remained lonely and isolated in the house. One Sunday an elderly woman (a cousin of ours) passed to visit me. She told me she thought about me that morning in church as she listened to the other girls singing in the choir. Looking at me with pity in her eyes she went on to say "Look at you just sitting there it would have been better for you to die". Die! The thought of dying had never crossed my mind. Even though I was suffering I had hopes for the future and to hear some one trying to dismiss that thought from my mind was too much for me. I decided there and then to fight harder to get better. After the woman left I got up and put that bad leg on the floor and stood on it. The pain was excruciating, but never the less I put my full weight on that leg and was determined not to succumb to being lame any more. This incidence brought about the beginning of my healing and I made myself a promise that I would never allow any one to take pity on me.

I do believe the word of God, which states:

"I can do all things through Christ which strengtheneth me".

(PHIL 4:13)

Therefore I would never allow any one to put me down, and make them succeed in saying I told you so.

With this thought in mind I was determined to succeed in this mission come what may.

5

WAYSIDE

God had been talking to us about finding premises and stated that the building is right under my nose, which gave me reason to believe that it's nearby. Again we prayed and asked him to send someone to show us where the building is situated. One day a lady that I knew came in whilst we were getting ready for fellowship. I asked her if she came to join us. She said that she had a house to rent and was about to go to the council with it when she had the urge to come to me.

I asked her where the property was and she said:

"In Dunlace Road",

"Can we rent it?"

She said: "Yes, but I didn't know you wanted to move from here."

Previous to her coming to me one night I had a dream in which I saw a multitude of people travelling on a very long road. These people had burdens on their heads, shoulders and their backs; they looked weary from their journey. As I looked there was nowhere for them to rest then at the far end of the road I saw one little house with a lantern burning. The name on the house was the Wayside Inn. God then said:

This house is for weary travellers to find rest and refreshments from their journey.

Mrs Joseph took me to see the house and imagine my surprise when I was taken into an end house on the road. After consulting the committee the decision was made to rent the property, and I promised to pay the two months fee within a few days. I had no idea where the funds would come from I only knew it would turn up on time and promptly signed. When it was Cathy, the vice chair's, turn to sign she suddenly realised we had no money and gasped out something to that effect. I quickly said it would be paid on Monday. God had showed himself true to his word once more, the funds were paid as promised.

We moved into the two-storey house in Dunlace Road in June 1992. We changed the name of the organisation to Wayside Christian Community Centre and became a non-sectarian organisation. We provided a preventative mental health service to the community in Hackney and the surrounding areas, and we operated an open door system where anyone in need could have access to available services whether Christian or non Christian.

Once more we had moved on without having any means of funding the project.

We went through some financial hardships and among other needs could not furnish the project efficiently.

However, God is faithful and provided more than enough tables and chairs for the dining and meeting rooms and for the office. We were able to purchase second hand office equipments and we quickly settled in. The worn out equipments were giving quite a lot of problems and prevented us from getting the work out as swiftly as we would like and I found myself occupying more and more of my time in the office. Finally, Vera suggested that we ask her son, Donald, and his friend Kevin to help out with the administration as they had IT skills. I also asked my two youngest Sons, Dean and Karvel, to help out and so between these four youngsters they helped us overcome the problems, and were the first volunteers recruited at Dunlace Road including my eldest son Michael and my grandchildren, Michael Jnr and Lareisse. By this time my husband and I were reconciled and he also played his part. Gradually, users became volunteers together with numerous others recruited from the community and from that time onwards volunteers were to become the backbone of the organisation. These include Pastor Cathy and Ann, outstanding volunteers who now represent the organisation in my absent. The dedication of our volunteers enabled us throughout the years to demonstrate our ability to prioritise needs and channel resources effectively.

Although we had no paid workers then, the organization was stable due in large part to the commitment shown by the volunteers who organised the activities of the center. Even with limited resources our track record was one of dedication, hard work and commitment in the face of insurmountable obstacles. We had managed to maintain and deliver a high level of service to our clients and maintain an organisation of high ethical standards and show that Wayside could be sustained at times when the organisation had been unable to fund posts. Managing entirely on volunteer support became one of our strengths, and it was to have a positive impact on the organisation enabling us later to obtain funding on that basis.

Our clients found a whole new world open up to them at Dunlace Road. They met people from all walks of life. On any one-day they could be socialising with a doctor, social worker, local government officer, pastor, poet, Barrister, certified accountant etc. These were people who came for spiritual healing and counselling and had met with the 'outcasts of society', who sat among them unnoticed for whom they were. As I watched these two groups mingle together it was not hard for me to see that Jesus Christ himself had initiated this project and had made it all possible for mentally ill people to be socially included in our society. Many of these young people would later on take up prominent positions in local government departments, train in business management, counselling and give lecture in schools and colleges in several London boroughs. What may be hard for man to achieve God can surely succeed in doing.

The athmosphere in the house was truly joyful. We had a keyboard and there were several African young men who found refuge among us. They developed friendships among the others, and taught us new songs, they played the keyboard, and guitar, there was dancing, singing and laughter. This activity was conducted every day after lunch and it was usually hard for us to leave by the end of the day.

We provided for this new clientele in the form of clothing and food. We asked the regular users to look out for bargains at the supermarkets and to purchase items of food on sale so that we could distribute to them and any other destitute people who dropped in. Through this small gesture people began to bring beverages, vegetables and even poultry. We also provided clothing for children and several young couples regularly received help.

Among the users was a wealth of skills and experiences and we began to put those talents to good use. First, the service users were invited to become members of the Executive committee where they could express their views and opinions. We did a skills analysis and then allotted tasks to everyone i.e. taking the register, doing the cooking, leading bible studies, fellowship, writing plays for our Caribbean evenings, collecting people in their car to bring them for prayer meeting etc. Among these were several of the mentally ill clients who were gradually being empowered and fitting back into society.

People cared for the welfare of each other and it was wonderful to see small groups of people either ministering to each other, comforting and encouraging one another, or just enjoying each others company. This setting was unique, it was a mixture of the whole community, young and old and the in between suffering mental ill health, blindness, depression, social isolation, rejection, They were refugees, the unemployed, people seeking political assylum, the broken hearted, the lonely, the bereaved and others

AWAY DAYS

Cliff College had become special to me since my conversion there and ever since then we hired a self-driven minibus and took a group of 14 people to a retreat weekend there. We spent many happy moments there learning to live with each other and knowing each other more.

Early mornings were spent either attending prayer meetings or walking along various prayer paths in meditation and prayer. Free times were spent in various ways like afternoon guided tours, strolls over the hills, sightseeing, visiting nearby villages and towns, market places, and churches. Although the young people we took were usually still on medication we felt the need to take them along so as to help their recovery and increase their confidence. It was marvelous to see how they interacted with other people and formed some lasting relationships with people from all over the country. God in his infinite wisdom had performed wonders for their health and we believe that these trips helped greatly.

We organised trips to the seaside and historical places such as Hastings, Brighton, Bournemouth, Eastbourne, Stratford-Upon-Avon etc. We even went occasionally to see plays at the theatre.

Local services were structured to meet the need of a few groups of people but here was the one place where all could be accommodated and cared for at the same time.

From the outside no one seemed to understand what the project was about but to those who came and benefitted: it was simple. Here was a place that catered for body, mind and spirit. This was achieved by them feeling truly loved, cared for and accepted for who they were and God did the rest. In simple terms people were finding a psychologically appropriate remedy that improved their condition. As people recupertated they were able to return to society and take up prominent positions in the community.

Around this time a young man by the name of Ian Rathbone turned up seeking support for a friend of his who was mentally ill. Ian volunteered to write to a local trust asking for funding on our behalf, through Ian the chairman of the trust made a visit to the organisation and witnessed first hand the work that was being carried out. That chairman was so inspired that he later advised us that the trust would release £1000.00 to the organisation every quarter for as long as we needed the funds. Several years later Ian would become a local government councillor and hold regular surgeries at Wayside and also become the Patron of the Organisation.

6

THE RESTRUCTURING OF THE PROJECT

The wider community gradually began to visit us to seek information. Many were fascinated by what they saw and heard. Among them were representatives from Age concern Hackney, and the Mental Health Locality Teams. We had applied to them for support previously but was unsuccessful because of the structure of the organisation. As mentioned previously people from various sections of the community integrated together as one group. At that time I played several roles within the organisation as there was no one else with the necessary skills needed to run an organisation. Therefore, I acted as manager, fundraiser, project Co-ordinator, Chairperson, counsellor, minister, etc. There were those who thought it was my duty to perform all the tasks because it was my ministry. However, I believed that no one could work on their own and that delegation and partnership was essential to building any organisation. Further, this was the way God had instructed me to go from the very beginning. However, because of the lack of resources I started out as best as I could but from reading the criterias in the funding applications forms I realised that the only way to access funding will be to develop projects in different categories. We found this very hard to do as we believed that people were happy just as they were but knew it was necessary.

And so as the mental health officials came they promised us funding if we dismantled the whole thing into smaller projects. So we restructured into several other projects as advised. Unknown to us we were to lose that intimacy forever with only memories to cherish for the rest of our lives.

Restructuring meant we faced more challenges. We couldn't work in isolation and if we were to be supported we would have to raise our profile. A Capacity building programme was advertised and we grabbed the opportunity and enrolled for a two-year course. This helped us put 12 policies and procedures in place and we received the Hackney Standards Awards Certificate from the mayor of Hackney along with the other groups who completed the training in 1996. Apart from this, we submitted an application for a part time finance/ administrative post and were successful and we employed our first paid worker that same year. We forged links with CANDL, a Barnardos Project working alongside churches to provide consultancy. We had worked with other consultants before but felt no effect under their leadership, but with CANDL this was very different, they saw the potential of the organisation and showed great interest in us. Not only did they make us feel appreciated they also encouraged us to tell our story to other organisations in an effort to give them hope in their struggles.

So with the help of CANDL and their expertise we produced our first business plan. This helped immensely to enable us to acquire funding from various Major Trusts and from Central Government funding sources.

HEALTH PROJECT

As a community project, and particularly with a high percentage of elders from the black community, Wayside was very concerned about promoting a healthy lifestyle for our users. Research had shown that there was a higher risk of the black population suffering from illnesses such as strokes, diabetes and high blood pressure than other sections of the community. In an effort to address this cause we got involved with Health Action Zone (HAZ Partnership). This project was developed to help improve the health of the community and Wayside has been a partner in the project from its conception. Apart from this we were the only church project committed to improving the health of the community.

Funding for the partners came from E.L.C.H.A (East London & City Health Authority) ours went towards a healthy living project incorporating Aerobics, Cooking Demonstrations, Health Awareness workshops and general advice for a period of three years. This project was of great benefit to various people who themselves had suffered the effects of strokes previously. The regular workshops were also beneficial and brought about great rewards in the restoration of people's health. Years later we will be able to deliver several health and fitness projects not only in Clapton but also around Hackney. This will have a great effect on the people and bring abundant blessings to the organisation as a whole.

7

THE DECLINE

So the organisation reached its peak in services and gradually began to decline. The unemployed found employment, the others became well and moved on, people emigrated to Africa and the Caribbean. Brother Steve, who faithfully collected people to bring to the weekly prayer meetings, lost his vehicle and could not continue. The majority of people lived outside walking distances, so this meeting also lost out. Applications submitted was unsuccessful, with all our funds depleted we were in big trouble. Unknown to ourselves at that time some of the reasons why we were turned down was because we were using a residential property for the project and no one was willing to give us rent.

We got deeper and deeper in debt for the rent. The landlady was very patient with us, as she had witnessed at first hand God at work through us. However, our situation worsened with less people in attendance by this time we were left with only six people meeting on a daily basis and not enough funds to pay our way.

We prayed and fasted - nothing happened. Every avenue we tried failed; yet, in all this struggle I clearly heard God saying:

"keep the door open if it's only one person attending".

I replied: "God that person will be very expensive to keep."

We decided to organise a jumble sale event. We publicised the event as much as we could even droping flyers in other areas as we felt certain that people would turn up, but on the evening only two people turned up. I was disappointed and heart broken and wept openly that evening. I did not care who was there. As far as I was concerned I was speaking to my heavenly father who knows all things well and if any one wanted to earsdrop on the conversation that was okay. So I wept and poured out my heart to God telling him of the frustrations, the hardships, the workload, the time and effort it took to organise the event and then failing to make it a success. I wept so much that at times I gasped for breath. I had tried everything now I'd come to a dead end. I could do no more, and then suddenly I felt overwhelmed with the love of God as he wrapped me tenderly in his heart causing me to rejoice as I've never done before. It was as though God was saying:

I do understand. I too feel your pain but all things work together for good for those who love God, who are called according to his purpose.

(ROMANS 8: 28)

The love that I felt was also poured out on the other sisters who joined me in rejoicing. All at once we found ourselves going up the stairs to the chapel where Thomas was heard playing the keyboard and we all joined in praise and worship to God.

In that moment of frustration I was reassured that all is not lost that God was very present in our situation and that he was able to get us through in his time.

We may not always understand why things happen as they do nevertheless I've learnt that nothing can stop God's constant presence with us.

Who shall separate us from the love of Christ? Shall tribulation, or distress, or persecution, or famine, or nakedness, or peril, or sword? Nay, in all these things we are more than conquerors through him that loved us.

(ROMANS 8: 35,37)

Looking back I realise that we must go through many trials and difficult situations if we are to truly have knowledge of God. Our task in life is not to succumb to situations and run away from them instead we are to overcome each one as they occur.

Christmas came and there were not enough of us to organise the usual Carol by candlelight event with the threat of eviction high on the agenda we were all broken hearted. One of the members cried: "God this can't be the end of Wayside." To which I respond: "No, by God's grace there will be other carol by candlelight events.

We returned after the Christmas break to the same situation, by now the bills were piling up and finally we had letters from the Bailifs to quit within a certain period of time. This was the time when God himself seamed to have left without leaving any forwarding address. All our efforts to communicate with God seemed futile; he did not speak neither did he act. Nevertheless, I never doubted his ability to intervene and I would constantly remind him of the promises he'd given me concerning the organisation.

A few months after starting the prayer meeting, in a vision,he had said:

"You don't know where this prayer meeting is going to lead you."

"Where can a prayer meeting lead." I asked, to which he said:

"All over the world"

On another occasion in a vision he had shown me vast numbers of people coming to the project. I was so overwhelmed by the multitude that I cried out God I'm only a woman how can I care for all these people?

Knowing God's purpose for the project kept me holding on even when it seemed there was nothing to hold on to; and I cried out: "

God please don't make my enemies triumph over me."

There were those who would have loved to see disaster coming our way. I would meet people who were surprised and disappointed to hear that our organisation was still running. These people and others would have been pleased to hear of our demise.

In obedience to God we continued to keep the door open and provide food as usual.

Because God had made that property available for us we couldn't see ourselves leaving there. We were comfortable, and particularly loved the house and the garden where we spent many happy hours socialising together. We didn't feel the need to relocate especially at a time when only a few people attended. However, God had something different in mind but this new venture would bring about doubt and test my faith as never before.

A few days after receiving the letter to quit, sister Vera asked me to prepare a special dish for the next day. I didn't feel up to attending the centre, but the next day I got up and heard a voice sending me to the estate agent in Chatsworth Road to ask for a commercial property.

I had gone to that same place before and knew that they deal only in residential properties. I was tired; feeling sorry for myself, and just wasn't in the mood to go on a wild goose chase. I left home that morning and decided to take another route to the centre that would prevent me from meeting too many people. I just did not feel like talking to any one. As I walked deep in thought I forgot where I was going and found myself walking towards the estate agents. I entered and told the lady sitting behind the desk what I was looking for. She told me they deal only in residential properties and didn't know of any other estate agents who specialised in commercial properties.

As I approached the door to leave she asked me to wait, as she had just remembered a Jewish man who was to purchase a property just up the road. She mentioned that he intended to let the shop front, and the first floor but intended to keep the top floor for himself. I explained that I needed the whole property for the project. I sat down and waited whilst she tried to contact him. He wasn't available so she left a message on the answer phone. I left that office feeling much better in myself knowing God was at work once again and that he will surely rescue us. This was a glimmer of hope and I quickened my steps and praised God for his intervention.

8

CHATSWORTH ROAD

A few days later I received a call from Mr Davis (the intended propieter) telling me that the contracts had not been exchanged as yet, but once the purchase is completed he would call. A couple of weeks went by before I received the call to meet him at number 24 Chatsworth Road. I met two gentlemen, one said he admired people who were doing something for their community especially a woman.

They showed me around the property and said if we wanted the property they would give us a lease of between 10 to 15 years renewable every four years, he would only ask for one month rent up front and one month in advance. He further said he will give us three months rent free period to clean up the premises, and that he will be responsible for repairing the outside of the property and we will be responsible for the internal. I told him we would like to take on the property, but wanted the committee members to see it. I knew nothing about this property and there was no indication that it was on the market for sale, as it was locked up for a considerable time. Furthermore, we had no money to pay the sort of deposit needed for a leasehold property. Yet, here I was negotiating for a property without two farthings to my name. Mr Davis had told me that another person was interested in the property. I believed this was an apportunity not to be missed and said we definitely will have the property.

He gave me the keys so that the others could see the property. He advised me to see a solicitor, so that the lease could be drawn up. I hurried back to the centre to communitcate the good news, without even thinking about where the money was going to come from. When I got there a lady whom we hadn't seen for a while was there waiting for me. She said that on her arrival she had heard about the property and was happy for us. I was so excited that I began to tell sister Vera about our good fortune and during this conversation the lady told us that she had already been to her bank and withdrew a monetary gift for the organisation. I could not believe my ears when she told us how much. It turned out that it was the exact amount needed to give to the landlords. I was reminded there and then of a hymn my great Aunt sang with gusto.

God moves in a mysterious way
his wonders to perform
he plants his footsteps in the sea
and rides upon the storm.

Judge not the Lord by feeble sence
But trust him for his grace
Behind a frowning providence
He hides a smiling face

His purposes will ripen fast
Unfolding every hour
The bud may have a bitter taste
But sweet will be the flower.

WILLIAM COWPER (HYMNS & PSALMS)

Over five years previously we were called to the bedside of a relative, of this same lady, who had a serious illness, and whom doctors had given over for dead. She had heard about us through a friend that found healing through our prayers.

We visited and prayed for the sick person and he survived. Now they remembered us by saying thanks.

All the people that were present at the centre went along with me to see the property. It was clear that they were disappointed with what they saw. The property had been locked up for several years and was in a bad state.

Broken/discarded shop fittings were piled on the floor and in the corners, all the ceiling panels in the shop had been removed, electrical fittings were pulled out, loads of garbage littered the entire floor and one may be excused for believing that the shop had been vandalised.

The carpets on the stairs were badly worn out and needed to be replaced. The first floor rooms were dark and dingy. The top floor ceilings leaked and the windows of the property were so shaky that when the wind blew I begged God to place his hands on them to keep them from falling and causing a fatal accident on the street below.

The outside building was equally in a mess two large buckets placed strategically on the ground told their own story and one only needed to look up and be reminded why they were precisely placed there. The outdoor make shift kitchen had a gaping hole in the roof and broken glass littered the floor - the entire place was an eye sore. There was no heating and everyone thought I had gone mad in believing that God would send us to such a dilapidated place. Some people thought the property was well beyond our capability to render any significant improvement that would allow proper use for the community. Too many things needed to be done and they felt they didn't know where to begin. I, however, thought we only needed to tidy the place then we could see the possibilities better.

The following day I set out to do battle with the grime with my nine year old grandaughter Lareisse, armed with three rolls of black bin bags, a broom and duster. With scarves on our heads and dressed in working clothes we marched up the road in broad day light looking like two witches. On entering the shop we rolled up our sleeves and began the attack. We pilled stuff into bags upon bags, removed large obsticles from the floor and tidied up as much as we could.

However, after two hours hard labour we accepted defeat and calmly surrendered.

Over lunch we decided to abandon the shop forever and start on the top floor, that would be easier as we may be able to succeed in cleaning one room at least. On reaching the top floor we surveyed the room to determine where to start. Lareisse looked at me with hopelesness in her eyes and said: "Nanny this place is very bad... she paused a little then continued by saying: but when it is finished it will be beautiful." With tears in my eyes I hugged her and said in agreement: "Yes it is bad but when it is finished it will be beautiful." With that thought in mind the two of us went to work and within a short time we were able to clear what is now the main office.

I'd been trying desperately to make the premises look more presentable for when the remainining members of the committee came. I had briefed everyone on the property by saying there was some work to be carried out. However those members who had seen it first hand had not shared my enthusiasm as they felt that nothing could be done to improve the property without having several thousands pounds to pay workmen to go in and do the work. In an effort to impress the others from having the same experience I'd decided to try and make it more impressive. You see in my understanding of the situation faced by the organisation I had to consider what was the greater of the problem whether it was to trust God and take on a property in that condition or to have no building at all. I do believe that God's understanding is not as man's we read :

For my thoughts are not your thoughts, neither are your ways my ways, saith the Lord. For as the heavens are higher than the earth, so are my ways higher than your ways, and my thoughts than your thoughts.

(ISAIAH 55:8-9)

I was not even going to try and understand why this property. All I was going to do is trust God for his grace.

By the end of the week the surrroundings looked much better apart from the obvious structural damage. The day came for the viewing. I felt the committee would see the potential of the property but it was not so. People went around silently, and when a comment was finally made it definitely was not encouraging. One new member voiced her opinion and commented: "We are Princes and Princesses and when God gives us something we expect it to be the best".

I asserted myself and responded by saying: "This is the best. When God created the world it was in chaos, but look at the beautiful world we live in today. God has plans for this place. I see beyond the chaos only sorry that I can't show you what I see but it will definitely become the place God has in mind. However, amid the scepticism they saw some truth in what was said and fully co-operated.

The time was approaching for us to move in, so we patched the carpets the best we could, bought a tin of paint and painted the wall paper in one of the first floor rooms, and the shop. By this time it was summer and people could be seen every where making improvements to their property, painting and decorating and so on. I said: "God you will help me I know, but it would take a severe unexpected happening and hard work to bring this about."

GOD'S PROVIDENCE

We decided to display a few items in the shop and began operating a charity shop and the drop-in where we could continue services in a limited way until we could renovate the property fully.

One evening a few of us was on the first floor when we heard a crashing sound. We all ran out to see what had happened. To our horror we discovered that several large chunks of masonary had fallen from the roof of our building and had made quite a mess on the pavement. Debris was everywhere and it was a miracle no one had been hurt. The crashing sound had brought all the shop keepers and nearby residents out to witness the disaster. After being rendered speechless, I got on the phone and called the fire brigade who arrived within minutes. They cordoned off the area and placed a sign saying dangerous structure. They instructed me to get in touch with the Local authority who would advise me on what to do next. We tried to contact the landlords but unfortunately the office was closed, In the meantime, the Council had erected some scaffolding and issued the landlords with a writ to fix the problem immediately after their return to the office.

By this time almost every one was on my case. People were criticising me personally for making a very bad and irresponsible decision. Knowing what was being said I held my head high and walked up the road each day talking to my God who knows all things well. Amid all the trying circumstances I never doubted that God himself had provided that particular property and somehow he would rectify the damages.

The Landlords contacted us after their return from holiday. They came with a builder to assess the damages and made an appointment for the work to be carried out as soon as possible. With the structural work in process the owners came and instructed me that they will be painting the outside wall and be replacing all the old windows with double glazing throughout.

We set about to seek fundraising and decided once again to apply to the community fund. They had turned us down twice previously, but we decided to try one more time. Pauline offered to help and took the lead in completing the forms whilst I worked on a further two applications for renovations.

After the applications were submitted we were contacted by a representative from Action for Employment. This government initiative worked in partnership with organisations/churches to give opportunities and equip young people for the job market. Organisations/churches would provide the work whilst Action for employment provides the materials and the trainees. After several formal meetings to determine our suitability and make an assessment of the work to be carried out they began the task of transforming the inside of the property.

Within months of starting the decorating project we received a call from the Community Fund informing us that our application was successful and that we were awarded the second largest grant in London the sum of £184,000.00 over three years for two office workers post, the purchase of office equipment and for the training of staff and volunteers. Two weeks later we received news that the other two applications were also successful bringing in another £30,000.00 for renovations to the property. The renovation grant enabled us to replace the ceilings in three rooms, install central heating throughout the property, renovate the kitchen, replace the roof of the outer building, erect a ramp and railings and erect an overhead covering so we could go from one building to the next without getting wet.

This new project meant that more youths came to work alongside the other professionals and develop even more invaluable skills. It was great to see the co-operation of the plumber, carpenter, electrician, plasterer and bricklayer working together in unity with the trainees.

With the work completed we had an Open Day in June 1999 in our newly refurbished building achieved just 16 months after signing the contract. This was a very memorable event, celebrated with members of the community and the young people from Action for Employment, and friends from as far away as Watford.

John Greenleaf wrote:

Who fathoms the eternal thought?
Who talks of schemes and plan?
The Lord is God!
He needeth not the poor device of man

Yet in the maddening maze of things
And tossed by storm and flood
To one fixed stake my spirit clings;
I know that God is good!

And if my heart and flesh are weak
To bear an untried pain,

The bruised reed he will not break
But strengthens and sustain

I know not what the future hath
Of marvel or surprise,
Assured alone that life and death
His mercies underlines.

JOHN GREENLEAF WHITTIER (HYMNS & PSALMS)

Our refurbished building has given more space enabling us to plan greater events and programmes.

We networked with organisations outside Hackney among them, Islington African/ Caribbean Elders group led by Pastor Desmie McLean. We organised a few Banquets together and Pastor McLean offered her hair dressing services at discount prices for the over 50's. She was also instrumental in the setting up of a Bible school here at Wayside under the leadership of Professor Sam Danuels of the Redeeming Voice Theological Institute (UK).

Jean Buffong and Desrenah Brown would later develop other projects to benefit the wider community at home and abroad.

We were able to promote healthy living programmes such as: three healthy cooking demonstration; twice weekly exercise classes, and our annual eye check with free spectacles for the over 50's who are diabetic, on income support or those with glaucoma.

For the first time we were able to focus specifically on men's health by holding a seminar on prostrate cancer. We also re-opened the luncheon club for the elderly.

A few years later we forged links with Inshape in Hackney. We provided much more classes for older people throughout the borough.

With the two new workers in post we set about promoting the services and soon referrals began to come through the mental health rehabilitation unit. They referred mainly refugees who were mentally ill from Sierra Leone, The Gambia, Congo and

Cameroon. We provided food and clothing to these refugees who were all Muslims but took part in the fellowship with us and loved the prayers and choruses. Friendships developed between us and the other mentally ill clients who helped them with their English.

Before relocating to this place we had developed ties with the Homerton Hospital, and we now worked in partnership to provide volunteers to transport patients to the hospital chapel for worship on Sundays. Two of the Chaplains had been regular visitors to the drop-in and they often brought along destitute people to collect food and clothing.

9

New Developments

CHARITY SHOP

From feedback gained through questionnaires. The need for a charity shop was highlighted to provide good quality clothing at affordable prices to satisfy the need to both parent and child.

Now that we had access to a shop front the opportunity to open a charity shop came to meet another need of the community.

This project has now grown into a multicultural user-friendly venue for people to meet, shop and simply have a chat in a non-threatening, safe environment. We have deliberately created an environment that is different from the ordinary shopping experience for members of the community to come at their leisure, and socialise whilst shopping. This has transformed the drop-in centre tremendously. Shoppers now have the privilege to sip tea, coffee and other beverages whilst being engaged in conversation with each other, which has brought tremendous transformation and self-development to individuals.

The project has enabled several people to develop skills from shop assistant to computer literacy. Recently, some customers asked for the opportunity to develop their vocabulary in English through volunteering. Three people have learnt to speak the language well enough to go on to further education. The shop is a buzz of activity uniting people of different cultures in one common goal of social inclusion.

The shop is also a valuable resource to members of the community. It provides products for people of all ages and backgrounds. Garments are available for weddings, funerals, interviews, parties, confirmation and every day wear.

A large selection of text books of various subjects, poetry, dictionaries, fiction, biographies, travel, cookery, childrens, christian books and bibles are in stock.

We have so many resources that we are constantly blessing others with gifts of clothing and books to help their ministries both here and overseas. We also provide large quantities of clothing to hospitals and organisations doing street work with the homeless.

It also provides some income helping us to become sustainable in the long term.

Wayside is proof that God can provide for all our needs. On entering our premises people are usually amazed at the services that are available for them. Prayer, counselling, bible study, advocacy, social and recreational activities, health & fitness classes, advice sessions, day trips to the theatre, sea side resorts and historical towns and villages, plus a place to shop.

OLD PEOPLES HOME OUTREACH

We visit an old peoples home regularly on Sundays to provide fellowship with the residents. I had worked at this particular home many years previously and had seen how other religious groups conducted fellowship there. In my observation they never tried to get the residents to interact, but were interested only in the staff. I decided that once we got on board things would be completely different. We would try to interest them to participate by singing choruses from sunday school days, and talk to them in between. When we first started the project, the residents showed little interest as some of them were confused, lacked concentration, and others talked to each other loudly during the meetings. However, as the weeks progressed there were changes in their behaviour - they talked less and showed interest in what was going on around them.

The more alert ones began to respond to the word of life. They shared memories of the past when they attended Sunday school and other church events, they chose hymns, and even offered prayers. We took it in turn to bring the message and felt at the end of each meeting a sense of great satisfaction.

THE SUNSHINE PROJECT

The regular users were moving on and new ones were being referred. Visiting clients in their homes opened up our eyes to the other plight suffered by the mentally ill person returning home from hospitals. We found them lying on unkempt beds in untidy rooms, most often the homes were in a bad state of disrepair, and the people themselves needed help with their personal hygiene.

On our visits we began to reach for the Hoover and help tidy up the best we could, we also combed the women's hair and had men volunteers shave and trim the men's hair. We provided curtains for windows and toiletries and began to look for ways to develop a project to meet this need. Help came in the form of an acquaintance, Desrenah Brown. She came to me with an idea she had for an outreach service that would help mentally ill people who were discharged from hospitals early whilst still needing care. The project idea was to provide practical support that would help clients cope better with everyday tasks and befriending. This included: volunteer support in accompanying clients to do the shopping, for walks in the park, to the hairdressers, the local market, or lonely people at home who would like to see a friendly face and people living on their own expecting a workman, but afraid to let a stranger into their home. The sunshine project would accommodate such a client.

We took the idea to professionals who thought it was a good idea. We then decided to submit a proposal to seek funding. The proposal was written up by Desrenah and sent to two funding agencies. We were successful and were able to employ another worker to set up the Sunshine Project for a period of four years. The project brought interest to the effect that referrals came from several agencies including Doctors,

Social workers, and Occupational Therapists from Hospitals, Statutory and Voluntary Agencies.

We were further inundated with calls from Careers and Referral Agencies such as Mental Health Locality Teams, Homeless Assessment and Resettlement Team, MIND, Living Space, Kadimah Centre (Jewish Care) and individuals, seeking befriending for relatives and clients who were isolated and in need of friendship.

As a result of our effort to provide this service we have witnessed some great transformation in the lives of our clients and have received letters of thanks from their relatives.

The volunteers usually report how rewarding and appreciative their visits are. How it gives them great pleasure to see the change in personality of each client people have become more tolerant to their family, relationships within the home is far less stressed since they regained some independence for themselves. Two people who received support recovered enough to offer friendship to others themselves.

Volunteers receive great satisfaction and fulfilment interacting with people in the community. They commented by saying: "It is rewarding to see the smile on someone's face during a visit", or to hear a client saying, "you can't take the pain away, but your company made my day". "After accompanying someone who would not otherwise step out door, to the hairdresser, take them back home, have a cup of tea then leave that person uplifted and cheerful, is a great satisfaction."

OVERSEAS OUTREACH PROJECT

As a caring organisation Wayside had been sending much needed goods to a number of countries. This idea came when I attended a convention in 1998 and was introduced to several pastors attending from the Caribbean and Africa. After hearing their stories of the poverty prevalent in their societies and the hardships faced by these pastors I was inspired to do something to ease the suffering of individuals in those countries. At this time we were being blessed with a vast amount of clothing, books, and other useful items. I invited two of these pastors to the centre and subsequently sent consignments of goods to help their ministries in Ghana and Jamaica. We have since sent medical supplies like incontinent pads, wheel chairs, walking sticks, and frames and so on to a hospital in St.Vincent, but it wasn't until the year 2000 that the project took on momentum. This followed a visit by our secretary Jean Buffonge to Gambia (West Africa). Jean was introduced to the community of Bulock and saw for herself the need for improvement to the Day care and nursery school. The dilapidated school had approximately 350 children who were being taught in two small classrooms. As a result sometimes up to 100 children crammed in a class while the others waited outside for their turn.

With the help of funds raised we were able to have a large school erected. The Day care and Nursery school now boast its own vegetable garden.... Bananas, cassavas, paw-paw, beans and so on. A marvellous achievement. With these products available the food supplied by the World Food Aid can last longer. Few years ago this was a different story. Where there was open space around the school perimeter now stands wall fencing keeping the children safe; where there were only two small classrooms, more classrooms and a small office now stands.

Later on the project extend to include two projects in Jamaica, three in Guyana. We also assist projects in Poland, India, Zimbabwe, and Cameroon.

In the year 2006 we helped to erect another school in Uganda, help to pay four teachers salary for a period of one year and send regular consignments of books, clothing and food there.

Wayside recognise that individuals need to help themselves and encourage self-help. Therefore, skilled people in both the Gambia and Uganda projects were used to erect the buildings demonstrating a degree of independence on their part.

At the beginning of the school year 2008, 86 children are on the register in the school in Uganda. We receive regular reports, which show they are all doing well in their studies and the school is a great blessing to the community.

With the exception of the Gambia all the other projects are with Christian organisations. This means Wayside is helping with the spread of the gospel in several nations.

Objectives:

To provide humanitarian assistance, including food, educational materials, non-perishable items, and cash assistance where necessary for the survival of underprivileged/needy communities.

Provide educational opportunities to orphans and destitute children.

Provide Medical items like walking aids to promote independence to the handicapped and other vulnerable people.

INSHAPE PARTNERSHIP

Our Health & fitness program is provided in partnership with, Inshape in Hackney.

Inshape is a partnership of seven registered charities working in Hackney to create local, affordable opportunities for people over the age of 50 to enable them to live healthy active and rewarding lives. The opportunity to become a partner occurred when one of the original organisations involved dropped out at the last moment. I knew nothing about this partnership previously neither had I met Jon who contacted me to ask if we could possibly come on board. Jon is the director of the lead partner organisation the Sharp End. He told me that the proposal had already been written up and that we would need to provide half the funds needed for the budget. If we decide he needed me to write up a project and send it together with a budget for five years funding. At this particular time we had very limited activities, we had no funds to contribute to this project but I thought this was an opportunity we could not miss. I found myself agreeing but stated that instead of a monetary contribution we would give volunteers in-kind support as part of the funds we needed to put forward. Jon agreed and put the final proposal through. In the meantime he sent me all the information on the other partners and their proposals. Within months Jon called to say the proposal was successful. In January 2004 the Inshape partnership came into being. Inshape partners now have over 1000 members. Together we provide physical exercise; benefits advice; complementary therapies; healthy living sessions; social activities and home safety checks in community halls, sheltered housing and GP surgeries.

The Wayside package currently provides care and support to older people that will contribute to their ability to remain independent, reduce circulatory diseases, obesity and diabetes through improving health via exercise opportunities, health information, cooking sessions related to health and to cultural issues such as art & craft. Service users have found the classes a great source for socialising and it has clearly helped them feel more confident about themselves. The programme has also seen vast improvement in the health and well being of its users, it has enable participants the chance to regain all or some lost abilities. Health complaints such as High Blood Pressure, Diabetics, Arthritis, Stroke and Heart Disease have become more controllable and people are now able to do much more for themselves.

We now provide four sessions to Local Authority old peoples homes. We also hold sessions in luncheon clubs, Libraries, and Day centres.

Through the sharing of resources and information among partners our health awareness workshops are facilitated by professionals from the TLC Stroke prevention Unit, Homerton University Hospital, Primary Care Trust, and Age Concern Hackney who have provided a number of talks including stroke prevention, diabetes, heart disease and stroke workshops. Apart from the workshops other activities include healthy cooking demonstrations and two day trips yearly.

This partnership has brought with it tremendous blessings to 'Wayside', by giving us opportunities we never dreamt possible. It has widened our demographics, boosts our fundraising abilities, provided staff/volunteers, and training for the executive committee, helped with extensive media coverage, and contributed to the promotion of services to the wider community.

Our commitment to the community has increased tremendously over the years enabling the possibilities of delivering high quality services. This effort shall continue its good deed in tackling major issues facing the community by providing the care and support that will help to bring changes in circumstances.

10

THE SUSTAINING POWER OF GOD

At the present time we continue to provide the space for meeting spiritual needs, and many are reaching out for this support in a very positive way. During the year troubled young people amongst others came to ask for guidance and prayer and found direction where they lacked previously. They were able to make decisions about their future and take more responsibility for their lives.

The fellowship, which is being held on Thursdays, continue to be one of the highlights of the week attracting people from various traditions and areas such as Walthamstow, Tottenham, East Ham and so on. Recently, we have seen an increase in attendances from the other projects, which show that prayer is a very significant part of the organisation.

We continue to reach out to the sick and distressed through the telephone offering guidance, hope, and friendship. We also visit lonely people in their homes or hospitals.

We have seen God changed the views of those who previously accused and condemned me. When they saw the effect the work of the organisation was having on members of the community they stopped throwing stones and many began to access the services and also referred others.

All broken ties were renewed and relatives were able to at last respond by saying: "Keep up the good work". I am assured that God is the author of this work. Through the pressures of running the organisation, the mental/physical fatigue, the financial instability, the malicious accusations suffered I know that I could not have succeeded had I gone out in my own strength to do this work. Too many things were against us but God always intervenes and made it all possible.

Wayside has come a long way from its humble beginnings based on prayer and has progressed to a well established and sort after organisation.

It gives me great pleasure to know that the years of hard work in developing the organisation is finally showing rewards. The project, which met a need for a specific community, now embraces not only this multi-cultural community, of Hackney, but the wider community as well.

It's good to acknowledge that throughout all the struggles of previous years the Lord remained faithful and has kept us thus far.

I remember hearing someone saying never doubt in the dark what God has revealed in the light. This thought has carried me throughout the times of deep despair when all around me seemed to be in chaos and I could not understand what was going on. Yet, it was in the crisis points of my life that God revealed himself most as Saviour, Sustainer, Comforter, Healer and friend. He has shown himself to be faithful at every point of my journey and I consider myself truly blessed to be called to this ministry.

It is my prayer that more people will become involved, and give of their time, talents/skills to the advancement of this mission.